William Draper Brincklé, Alfred Hoffy

Hoffy's North American Pomologist

William Draper Brincklé, Alfred Hoffy

Hoffy's North American Pomologist

ISBN/EAN: 9783337107550

Printed in Europe, USA, Canada, Australia, Japan

Cover: Foto ©ninafisch / pixelio.de

More available books at **www.hansebooks.com**

HOFFY'S
NORTH AMERICAN POMOLOGIST,

CONTAINING NUMEROUS

FINELY COLORED DRAWINGS,

ACCOMPANIED BY LETTER PRESS DESCRIPTIONS, &c.,

OF

FRUITS OF AMERICAN ORIGIN.

EDITED BY

WILLIAM D. BRINCKLÉ, A. M.—M. D.,

Member Pennsylvania Horticultural Society; Corresponding Member Massachusetts Horticultural Society; Honorary and Corresponding Member New Haven County Horticultural Society, Buffalo and Southern Iowa Horticultural Societies; Honorary Member Wilmington Horticultural Society, &c., &c

PREPARED AND PUBLISHED BY A. HOFFY,

No. 1534 Vine Street, Philadelphia, 1860.

BOOK No. I.

FAIR OF THE AMERICAN INSTITUTE,
New York, Oct. 23rd, 1841.

A. Hoffy, Esq.—My dear Sir—I am happy to inform you that the "Orchardist's Companion" has been awarded a *Silver Medal,* and also recommended to special notice, which will be made public, &c.

Very respectfully yours,

T. DUNLAP.

I will here make an extract or two, from the numerous encomiums of the press, which appeared at the time, deeming them appropriate to this occasion.

"The '*Orchardist's Companion,*' we have examined with careful interest—we conceive that a publication of this kind is greatly needed, and that the extension of it is the best possible means of promoting the culture of fine fruits, and insuring success to the labor bestowed. The publisher is Mr. A. Hoffy, who edits the work, &c."—*National Gazette.*

"The '*Orchardist's Companion.*'—This beautiful and valuable work has just appeared, and is embellished with some of the most superb colored engravings of fruits we have ever seen—*no work of the kind has ever appeared in this Country,* and from the ability shown in the editorial management and the superior character of the plates, it cannot fail, we think, of creating no ordinary sensation. The whole work is got up in a very superior manner, and apart from its utility as a work of reference, it is a most beautiful ornament for the *centre-table.*"—*Saturday Chronicle.*

It was now suggested to me by Dr. Brinckle, to publish a Pomological work solely on our Native Fruits, in which new enterprise I gladly embarked, after he had in the first instance kindly consented to give me his editorial services, provided I received them gratuitously, and we gave it the title of the "American Pomologist." Unfortunately the whole edition of this valuable work was subsequently consumed, uninsured, in the conflagration of the Artisan Building, in Ranstead Place.

All the Fruits figured in the North American Pomologist, are from choice and well cultivated specimens of full growth and luxuriance, showing to what perfection they can be brought when the trees are raised with proper care and attention.

The North American Pomologist, not being a local work, nor connected with any Horticultural or Pomological Society, Establishment, or Association, contributions of native or seedling fruits, their histories, properties, descriptions, &c., are respectfully solicited, and for which due credit will always be given in the work to each contributor.

Dr. J. R. Shreve having, from pure zeal in the cause, connected himself with this work, it is particularly requested that all communications in relation thereto be addressed to him or to me.

The North American Pomologist will be published from time to time in books, neatly bound in muslin, each to contain thirty-six distinct pages of different *Native Fruits,* with full letter press descriptions, histories, &c., accompanying.

Each book will be complete in itself and independent of the other, so that purchasers will be enabled to suit their own views and tastes, without the necessity of going beyond the purchase of one book, when not deemed expedient—not more than three will be published in the whole, unless a fourth should afterwards be called for.

Respectfully,

A. HOFFY.

PHILADELPHIA, *May,* 1860.

NORTH AMERICAN POMOLOGIST.

EDITOR'S PREFACE.

The repeated disappointments which have attended the cultivation of Foreign Fruits in this country, render it daily more manifest that our chief reliance must be placed on those of native origin. Though many of the trans-atlantic varieties possess undoubted merit, and richly deserve all the praise bestowed on them, a still greater number are of inferior quality, at least when fruited in this country—and of those that are of a high order of excellence, some are shy bearers, and others are constitutionally too tender to withstand the great and sudden vicissitudes of our variable climate.

The design of the present work is to direct the attention of Horticulturists more prominently to our native fruits, and to give such a pomological description and colored drawing of them, as that they may be readily identified. Nothwithstanding some of our indigenous kinds have been long known, and quite extensively cultivated in some parts of our country, yet, they will be introduced into the work, not only to place them on record, but to enable the Pomologist, who may not be familiar with them, to discriminate the genuine from the spurious.

Many of our native fruits possess great excellence, and not a few of them will successfully compete with the most celebrated kinds from the eastern hemisphere. Among these we may mention the Seckel, Dix, Pratt and Columbia Pears. The Newtown Pippin, Fall Pippin, Rhode Island Greening, Esopus Spitzenberg and Northern Spy Apples. The Heath Cling, Druid Hill, Crawford's Late and Susquehanna Peaches. Lawrence's Favorite, Washington, Columbia and Jefferson Plums. Wendell's Mottled Bigarreau, Downer's Late, Coe's Transparent, and Dr. Kirtland's New Cherries, &c., &c.

Most of our domestic fruits are accidental seedlings—valuable varieties have also been obtained by planting the seed of the best known kinds. But when artificial fertilization during implanescence is resorted to, and the parents selected with judgment, a successful result is just as certain as that attending the similar course pursued in raising fine animals.

In conclusion, the Editor will embrace this opportunity to state that he is in no way connected with the profits and emoluments of the present undertaking. Having known Mr. Huffy for many years, and believing him to be a worthy man, as well as an accomplished artist, the undersigned desires most cordially to promote the enterprise, and with this view, his editorial services are rendered without any remuneration whatever. The propriety of addressing directly to the publisher, all communications in relation to the work, will therefore be apparent.

W. D. BRINCKLÉ, M. D.

PHILADELPHIA, MAY, 1860.

From Nature by A. Hoffy.

PENELOPE PEACH.

Synonym—Baxter's, No. 2.

Size—2$\frac{7}{10}$ inches long by 2$\frac{7}{10}$ broad.

Form—Roundish.

Suture—Distinct at the crown and at the apex.

Skin—Greenish White, slightly stained with red on the sunny side.

Cavity—Open.

Flesh—Greenish White, juicy, slightly stained at the stone, to which it does not adhere.

Stone—1$\frac{3}{4}$ inches long, 1 inch wide, and 1$\frac{1}{2}$ thick, deeply and slightly furrowed on the same stone; some of the ridges are quite acute, while most of them are rounded.

Flavor—Rich and delicious.

Quality—"Very good."

Maturity—Middle of September.

HISTORY, ETC.

This fine Peach originated with Mr. Isaac Baxter, the well known Philadelphia Pomologist, and was named by him after one of his daughters.

From Nature by A.Boff.

CHELTENHAM

CHELTENHAM.

Synonyms—Calf pasture.
Size—Medium, 2½ inches long by 2⅜ broad.
Form—Roundish.
Skin—Profusely striped and marbled with red on a yellow ground.
Stem—¼ of an inch long by 1/16 thick, inserted in a narrow cavity.
Calyx—Small, closed, set in a narrow, rather deep basin.
Core—Medium.
Seed—Brown, small, short, plump, ⅜ of an inch long, ¼ wide, ⅛ thick.
Flesh—Whitish yellow, tender, juicy.
Flavor—Pleasant.
Quality—"Good."
Period of Maturity—Middle of September.
Leaf—1 1/16 inches wide by 1½ long, including petiole, which is 11/16 of an inch long by 1/16 wide.
Wood—Young shoots greyish brown.

HISTORY, ETC.

The Cheltenham Apple originated in Cheltenham Township, Montgomery County, Pa., in a field in which the calves were usually pastured, hence the name *Calf pasture*, by which it is most commonly known. The tree has been in bearing over twenty-five or thirty years. The handsome appearance of the fruit adds much to its marketable value. Though not ripe till September, yet as early as July it may be used for culinary purposes.

From Nature by A Hoffy

DIANA.

Synonyms—None.
Bunch—4½ inches long, 3 wide; rarely shouldered; compactly set.
Berry—Size, rather smaller than the Catawba, from ¾ inch to 1½ in diameter.
Form—Round.
Skin—Pale red.
Seed—½ inch long, $\frac{3}{16}$ wide, ⅛ thick, light greyish cinnamon.
Flesh—Less pulpy and more juicy than the Catawba.
Flavor—Somewhat similar to the Catawba, but more delicate, and more saccharine.
Quality—"Best."
Maturity—A week or ten days earlier than the Catawba.
Leaf—Very similar to that of the Catawba.
Wood—Light brown.

HISTORY, ETC.

The Diana Grape originated with Mrs. Diana Crehove, of Milton Hill, near Boston, Mass.; from seed of the Catawba, planted nearly a quarter of a century ago. It fruited in 1838 for the first time, and in 1844 the attention of Pomologists was particularly directed to it by Mr. Hovey, in his Magazine of Horticulture. Independently of its intrinsic excellence, its early maturity peculiarly adapts it to the climate of the Northern and Eastern States, where the Isabella and Catawba seldom come to perfection, and further south, it is even better than at the North.

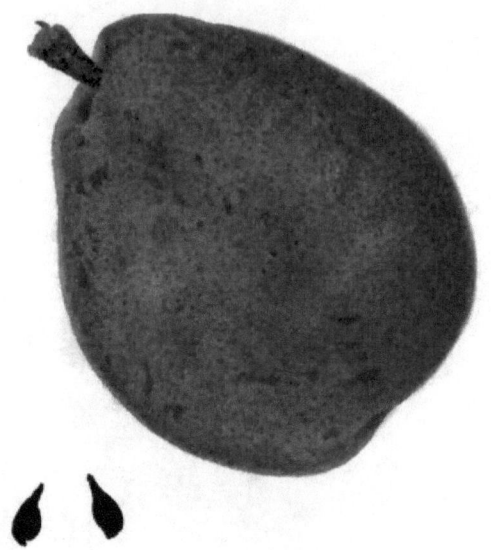

From Nature by A. Hoen

CHANCELLOR.

Synonyms—Green's Germantown—Early St. Germain.
Size—Large, 3¼ to 4 inches long by 2¾ to 3 broad.
Form—Long, obovate, inclining to pyriform.
Skin—Dull green, rough with numerous green and russet dots, some russet markings and occasionally a faint speckled, warm brownish cheek.
Stem—¾ to 1 inch long by $\frac{1}{12}$ thick, inserted sometimes by a fleshy termination into a small irregular cavity, usually elevated on one side.
Calyx—Small, open, set in a plaited shallow basin.
Core—Medium.
Seed—⅔ of an inch long, ¼ wide and ⅓ thick, of a yellowish brown color, acuminate, full at the obtuse end, on one side of which is a small angular projection.
Flesh—Fine texture, buttery.
Flavor—Rich and exceedingly agreeable, some may consider it saccharine, which in our opinion should never be viewed as an objectionable feature, since the saccharine quality is the first to show its deficiency in defective soils, unpropitious seasons or under poor cultivation.
Quality—"Very good" if not "best."
Maturity—Last of September and October. It keeps well and ripens handsomely without decaying at the core.
Leaf—Lanceolate.
Wood—Young shoots yellowish brown, slender.
Growth—Rather spreading.

HISTORY, ETC.

This truly delicious pear, probably a natural cross between the white Doyenne and St. Germain, originated at the country residence of Wharton Chancellor, Esq., on School House Lane, Germantown. The original tree still stands on his premises, within an enclosure of ever-greens, and is probably more than sixty years old.

Specimens of the fruit from a grafted tree in the garden of Mr. Joseph Green, of Germantown, were for the first time exhibited at the Annual Fair of the Pennsylvania Horticultural Society, in September, 1848; and to this variety was awarded the premium offered by the Society for the best seedling pear exhibited in 1849.

The first description of the Chancellor was published in the Horticulturist, vol. 3, page 567. This variety succeeds well on the quince.

CLEAVINGER.

Synonyms—None.

Size of Fruit—Large. { Longitudinal diameter, 2¼ to 2¾ inches.
Transverse diameter, 1¾ to 2 inches.

Form—Oval, sometimes obovate, with a wide superficial suture, extending from the base to the apex.

Skin—Dark purple, densely covered with bloom, which imparts to it a blue color.

Stem—½ inch long, ⅛ thick, inserted in a narrow depression, in which is a fleshy ring.

Stone—Rough, unadherent, perforate like that of the Moorpark Apricot. 1¼ inches long, 1⅛ wide, ⁷⁄₁₆ thick.

Flesh—Yellowish, parting freely from the stone.

Flavor—Mild and pleasant.

Quality—"Good at least, if not very good."

Maturity—Middle of August.

Leaf—Dark green, under surface glaucous, serrate-crenate, 3 inches wide, 4¼ long, including petiole, which is ⅞ inches long, ⁄. thick, and grooved.

Wood—Young shoots cinereous.

Growth—Vigorous.

HISTORY, ETC.

The Cleavinger Plum is a native of Pennsylvania. It originated in Philadelphia with Mr. Fernsler, from the stone of an unnamed Seedling variety, and was brought into notice by Mr. Wm. S. Cleavinger of West Philadelphia.

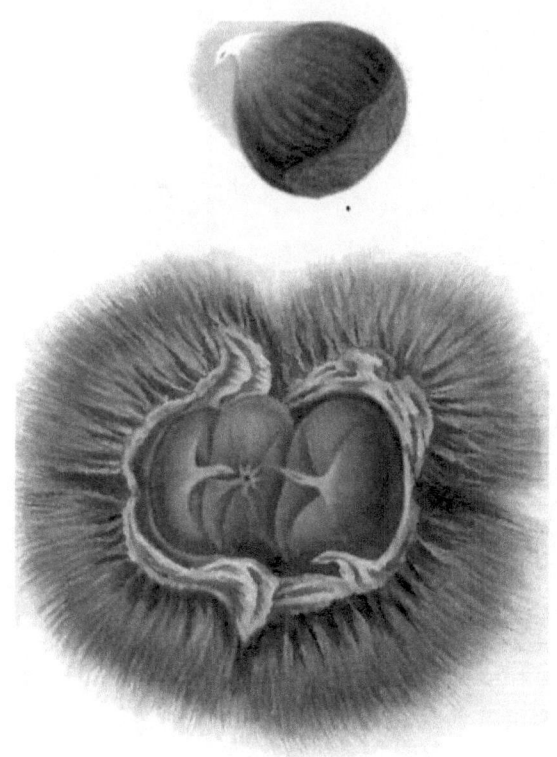

From Nature by A. Hoffy.

WILMINGTON CHESTNUT.

Synonyms—

Size of Nut—1½ inches long, 1¼ wide, ⅞ thick.

Form—Very similar to that of the common American Chestnut.

Skin—Of the ordinary chestnut color.

Flavor—Scarcely inferior to the American, but rather coarser in texture.

Quality—"Very good."

Maturity—Last of September and beginning of October.

Leaf—Large, deeply serrated, 2⅝ inches wide, and 7 long, including petiole, which is ⅞ inch long by ⅛ thick.

Wood—Young shoots, reddish brown, with many grey dots, old, greenish brown.

Bud—Short, round, full.

Growth—Very vigorous.

HISTORY, ETC.

The Wilmington Chestnut originated near Wilmington, Delaware, more than 40 years ago, from a nut of the Spanish variety, planted by my late father, Dr. John Brincklé. It usually reproduces itself from seed, and is a rapid and vigorous grower, hardy, and a uniform and most abundant bearer. These qualities, combined with its large size, render it eminently worthy of more extensive cultivation. In market it commands two or three times the price of the ordinary American Chestnut.

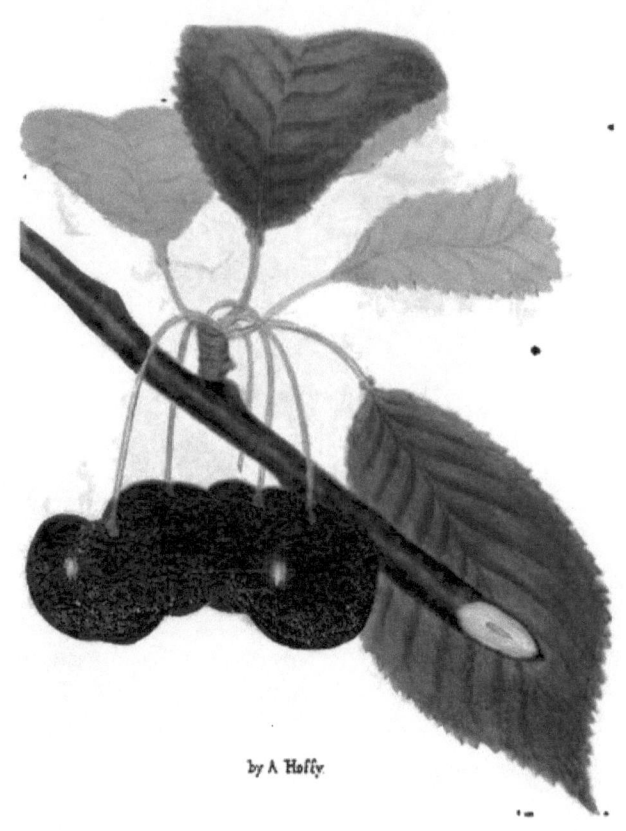
by A. Hoffy.

WENDELL'S MOTTLED BIGARREAU.

Size—Large, usually an inch in its transverse diameter.

Form—Obtuse heart shape, uniformly regular with a distinct and well marked suture extending half way around the fruit.

Skin—Rich dark purplish red, beautifully mottled with small points and streaks of a darker hue, which become quite indistinct when the fruit is fully ripe, the color then becoming nearly black.

Stem—About an inch and a half long, rather stout, and set in a round depression of moderate depth.

Seed—Small.

Flesh—Deep crimson, firm, crisp though not tough, and well supplied with a rich delicious juice.

Flavor—Rich, saccharine, and very agreeable.

Maturity—At Albany from the 7th to 15th of July, about the time of Downer's late red.

HISTORY, ETC.

This new, rich and beautiful native Cherry, originated from a seed of the Graffion or yellow Spanish, planted by Dr. Herman Wendell, of Albany, at his place near that city, in the Spring of 1840. It bids fair to take a high rank among the lovers of this favorite fruit. At the show of the Albany and Rensellaer Horticultural Society in 1849, it took the premium as the best variety exhibited, though it had to compete with the Black Tartarean, Graffion, Holland Bigarreau, Elton and others of merit, which were shown at the same time.

For the Pomological description of this fine Cherry, we are indebted to the kindness of our esteemed friend, Dr. Wendell.

BURLINGTON APRICOT.

Size—Medium to large.

Form—Oblong, somewhat compressed at the sides with distinct suture.

Skin—Golden yellow, with numerous red spots and a ruddy tint on the side exposed to the sun.

Flesh—Yellowish.

Stone—Yellow, moderately rough, perforated; in five stones out of twenty the perforation was entirely laid open, forming a furrow.

Flavor—Fine.

Maturity—From the middle of July to the beginning of August.

Blossom—Large.

Leaf—Large, broadly heart-shaped, terminating abruptly in a point and slightly serrated.

Wood—Reddish, old bark rough.

Tree—A vigorous grower.

HISTORY, ETC.

The Burlington Apricot originated from a seed of the Peach Apricot, planted by Mrs. Sarah Woolman, in 1838. In the Spring of 1842, the tree was removed to its present locality on the premises of her son, Mr. John J. Woolman, opposite the Lyceum, on the east side of Main Street, in Burlington. It stands on the south side of a brick house exposed to the east and west winds. The soil is a poor gravel thrown out in digging the cellar of the mansion.

The tree fruited for the first time in 1843, and in 1848 the fruit was exhibited before the Pennsylvania Horticultural Society.

For the history of this fine Apricot, I am indebted to the kindness and attention of David Landreth, Esq., of this city, and Samuel R. Wetherill, of Burlington.

From Nature by A. Hoffy

SECKEL.

SECKEL.

Synonyms—Seckle, Sickel, Syckle, New York Red Cheek.
Size of Fruit—{ Longitudinal diameter, $2\frac{2}{16}$ inches.
Transverse diameter, $2\frac{1}{16}$ inches.
Form—Obovate, often obconic.
Skin—Yellow russet, with frequently a mottled red cheek.
Stem—$\frac{2}{16}$ inch long, $\frac{1}{8}$ thick, inserted usually in a small depression.
Calyx—Small, closed, set in a small shallow basin.
Core—Medium.
Seed—Dark brown, $\frac{3}{8}$ inches long, $\frac{1}{16}$ wide, $\frac{1}{8}$ thick.
Flesh—Yellowish white, fine texture, buttery, melting.
Flavor—Rich, luscious, saccharine, highly perfumed.
Quality—"Best."
Maturity—Middle of September.
Leaf—$1\frac{11}{16}$ inches wide, $3\frac{1}{4}$ long, including petiole, which is $\frac{3}{8}$ inch by $\frac{1}{16}$ thick.
Wood—Young shoots olive, stout, short.
Growth—Moderate, forming a rounded symmetrical head.

HISTORY, ETC.

The Seckel is a native of Pennsylvania. The Horticulturist for January, 1849, contains the following description of the original tree in 1848:

"This venerable tree stands in a meadow in Passyunk Township, less than a quarter of a mile from the Delaware river, opposite to League Island, not more than half a mile from the mouth of the Schuylkill, and about three and a half miles from the City of Philadelphia. The property on which it stands is a portion of the Girard Estate, and now belongs to the city. It is one of the largest Seckel Pear trees I have ever seen, measuring more than six feet in circumference one foot above the ground, and four feet nine inches in circumference five feet higher up. It is about thirty feet high. The head of the tree has the usual rounded appearance so characteristic of this variety, and is in good condition. The trunk to the height of six feet, is very much decayed on its south-western side. The bark half way round the trunk is entirely gone, together with a great portion of the wood itself, leaving a large hollow in the tree. Such being the decayed condition of the trunk, it is greatly to be feared that the tree will not be able to stand the blasts of many more winters. No artificial support having been afforded to enable it to resist the dreaded effects of the stormy winds, nature herself is making an effort to provide for the anticipated disaster, by throwing up shoots from the trunk an inch or two above the surface of the earth. But the tree stands on grazing ground, and unless protected by an enclosure, the effort will prove a vain one."

The proper authorities having had their attention called to the exposed condition of this tree by the writer of the above, have caused the necessary protection to be given to it. This tree must be more than one hundred years old, as fruit from it was eaten by the late Rt. Rev. Bishop White, between eighty and ninety years ago.

NORTH AMERICAN POMOLOGIST.

From Nature by A. Hoffy

CLYDE BEAUTY.

Synonyms—Mackie's Clyde Beauty.
Size of Fruit—{ Longitudinal diameter, 2½ to 3¾ inches.
{ Transverse diameter, 2½ to 3½ inches.
Form—Conical, sometimes ribbed.
Skin—Striped and mottled with red on a yellow ground.
Stalk—Very short, ½ inch long, 1-7 thick, occasionally a fleshy excrescence on one side, inserted into a deep, rather wide furrowed cavity.
Calyx—Small, closed, set in a moderately deep angular basin.
Cone—Large, hollow.
Seed—Small, brown, ⅜ inch long, 1/16 wide, ⅛ thick.
Flesh—Fine texture, tender, juicy.
Flavor—Pleasant, sprightly, sub-acid.
Quality—"Very good."*
Maturity—October to December.
Leaf—2½ inches wide, 6 long, including petiole, which is 1½ inches long, 1/12 thick.
Wood—Young shoots, reddish brown, old, grey.
Growth—Vigorous, forming a fine spreading head.

HISTORY, ETC.

The Clyde Beauty is a native of New York. It was brought into notice by Mr. Matthieu Mackie, of Clyde, Wayne County, where it originated on the premises of his father.

---

* In compliance with the suggestion of Mr. A. J. Downing and others, the quality of the fruits described in this work will hereafter be more definitely expressed, by adopting the grades of merit recommended by the National Congress of Fruit Growers. These grades are "good," "very good," "best."

Drawn from nature by A. Hoffy.

HEATHCOT

HEATHCOT.

Synonyms—Gore's Heathcot.
Size—Medium, 2$\frac{7}{8}$ inches long, 2$\frac{7}{8}$ inches wide.
Form—Obovate.
Skin—Greenish yellow, with a few russet dots and streaks.
Stem—Rather long, and somewhat stout, $\frac{7}{8}$ of an inch long, $\frac{1}{8}$ thick, curved, inserted in a small russeted cavity.
Calyx—Partially closed, set in a shallow basin.
Core—Above medium.
Seed—Dark brown, long, acuminate, with a point or angle at the obtuse end, nearly on a line with the longitudinal axis.
Flesh—White, fine texture, buttery.
Flavor—Rich, vinous and perfumed, not unlike that of the White Doyenne.
Quality—"Very good."
Season of Maturity—Last September to middle of October.
Leaf—Oval-acuminate, usually folded and recurved, 1$\frac{3}{8}$ inches wide, 4$\frac{1}{4}$ long, including petiole, which is 1$\frac{3}{8}$ inches long, $\frac{1}{8}$ thick.
Wood—Young shoots, brownish olive; old, dark ferruginous.
Growth—Upright, with a bushy head.

HISTORY, ETC.

The Heathcot Pear originated from seed planted by Mr. Heathcot, who was at the time a tenant on the farm of Governor Gore, in Maltham, Mass. It came into bearing in 1824, and is probably a seedling of the White Doyenne, which it nearly equals in quality. This variety is a good and regular bearer; when the tree came to maturity it was introduced to the notice of pomologists by the late Jonathan Winship, Esq., of Brighton. Does not succeed well on quince.

From Nature by A. Hoffy.

NORTHERN SWEET

NORTHERN SWEET.

Synonyms—Golden Sweet, Northern Golden Sweeting.
Size of Fruit—Above medium. { Longitudinal diameter, 2¼ to 2¾ inches.
Transverse diameter, 3 to 3¼ inches.
Form—Roundish or truncate, ovate, sometimes obscurely ribbed.
Skin—Fair, smooth, golden yellow, with sometimes a crimson cheek.
Stem—½ inch long by ⅙ thick, usually curved, inserted into a moderately wide cavity, which terminates somewhat abruptly.
Calyx—Small, closed, set in a rather deep open plaited basin.
Core—Below medium.
Seed—Light chestnut, ⅜ inch long, ⅙ wide, ⅛ thick.
Flesh—Whitish, fine, tender, crisp, juicy.
Flavor—Saccharine, with an agreeable aroma.
Quality—" Very good."
Maturity—October and November.
Growth—Moderate, branches drooping.

HISTORY, ETC.

The Northern Sweet is believed to be a native of Vermont. It was brought into notice by Mr. Jonathan Battey, of Keeseville, Clinton County, New York. He gives in the Fourth Volume of the Horticulturist, the following history of this variety:—"Some 50 or 60 years ago, Nathan Lockwood, of Westchester County, New York, on his removal to St. George, Chittenden County, Vermont, took with him, as usual in such cases, seeds from which he raised trees and planted an orchard. In this orchard stood the tree, from which all others of this variety, so far as my knowledge extends, have been derived." Mr. Battey exhibited specimens of this Apple at the meeting of the Congress of Fruit Growers in 1849, which were favorably noticed in the Report of the Native Fruit Committee. The Northern Sweet comes early into bearing, and is said to be very productive. It is cultivated to a considerable extent in the valley of Lake Champlain, and has recently been widely disseminated by Mr. Battey.

From Nature by A Hoffy.

GENERAL HAND PLUM

GENERAL HAND.

Synonyms—Miller.
Size of Fruit—{ Longitudinal diameter, 2⅗ inches.
Transverse diameter, 2¼ inches.
Form—Roundish-oblong or truncated, oval.
Skin—Greenish yellow, broadly striped and marbled longitudinally with yellowish green, suture distinct, extending beyond the apex.
Stalk—⅝ inch long, ⅛ thick, often curved, inserted in a wide shallow cavity.
Stone—1 inch long, ¾ wide, ½ thick, rough, minute excavations, deep groove from base to apex on one edge, free, sometimes partially adherent at the edges.
Flesh—Yellowish, somewhat coarse, moderately juicy.
Flavor—Mild and pleasant.
Quality—"Good."
Maturity—Last of August.
Leaf—3½ inches wide by 5¾ long.
Wood—Young shoots greyish green, pointed buds, old wood grey in longitudinal stripes.

HISTORY, ETC.

The General Hand Plum is believed to be a native of Pennsylvania. Dr. Eli Parry, of Lancaster, Pennsylvania, has published in the 1st Vol. of the Pennsylvania Farm Journal, the following historical notice of this variety. "As my object in this communication is to endeavor to establish beyond a doubt, that the plum called the General Hand Plum, first received that name in the County of Lancaster, and not in Maryland. I called on Mrs. Brien, of our city, a daughter of the late Gen. Edward Hand, from whom I learned that he took great pains in collecting and cultivating choice fruit trees. She remembers his planting a number of small plum trees, but she cannot tell where he got them. Plums were very rare in this vicinity at that time. She also suggested that I might learn something further relative to the matter, by calling on Mr. Benedict, an aged and respectable citizen of our place, who informed me that in the autumn of 1791, he assisted in plastering the mansion house of the late General Hand, on the Conestogo, about one mile south-east of Lancaster; and he remembers that the plum trees were planted before that time; but that they were still quite small, and had not borne any fruit—he said that George Wein procured some grafts from the tree on General Hand's place, and gave Mr. George Miller, the present clerk of the Lancaster market, some of them. I called on Mr. Miller and he told me that in 1810 or 1811, Mr. George Wein procured about a dozen grafts from General Hand, (who was always very liberal to his neighbours in such matters,) and gave him two of them at his request; one, a young shoot, the other a year old piece with one lateral bud on it—and that one grew, but threw out no lateral branches that season—Mr. Wein was not so fortunate—none of his grew; and the following spring he applied to Mr. Miller for grafts, which he declined, giving as a reason the fact, that he could not cut off any grafts without spoiling his tree. During the second summer, there had been some lateral branches thrown out, and Mr. Miller furnished Mr. Wein with a few of them; but he was equally unfortunate in his second attempt to propagate them. That summer the *parent tree* died to the ground, so that in 1812 or 1813, we find all that beautiful variety of fruit concentrated in one little stalk, grown from the lateral bud on one of the grafts given to Mr. George Miller by Mr. Wein. From that circumstance, they were for a time called the "Miller Plum," until Mr. Miller objected to that name, and said that it was General Hand's Plum. From that time to the present they have been so called. Some years afterwards, Mr. Emanuel Carpenter procured some cuttings from Mr. Miller, and succeeded in propagating them, and as he told me, sent them to his brother in Ohio, to Mr. Sinclair, in Baltimore, and others. Thus it appears to me that some pomologists have improperly given Baltimore the credit of the nativity of this superb plum, which properly belongs to Lancaster County, Pennsylvania.

From Nature by A. Hoffy

JANE.

Synonyms—Baxter's, No. 1.
Size—Full medium, 2¼ to 3⅜ inches long by 2¼ to 3⅜ wide.
Form—Roundish, oblate.
Skin—Greenish yellowish white, with an unprepossessing dull green appearance on the shaded portion, and faintly stained with red on the exposed side.
Suture—Narrow, superficial, extending beyond the apex.
Cavity—Open.
Apex—Rounded.
Stone—1⅜ inches long, 1⅛ wide, ⅞ thick, deeply furrowed with rounded ridges.
Flesh—Greenish white, stained at the stone, from which it freely separates, very juicy.
Flavor—Rich and saccharine.
Quality—"Very good."
Maturity—Middle of September.
Leaf—4½ inches long, 1⅜ wide; petiole ₁⁴⁄₆ inches long, ₁⁄₆ thick; serratures crevate.
Glands—Globose.
Wood—Young shoots green on the shaded side, reddish on that exposed to the sun.
Growth—Vigorous.

HISTORY, ETC.

This variety is a native of Pennsylvania, having originated a few years ago with Mr. Isaac Baxter, of Philadelphia. It has been repeatedly exhibited at the meetings of the Pennsylvania Horticultural Society. At the meeting of the American Pomological Society at Philadelphia, in September, 1852, it was tested by the Native Fruit Committee, and decided to be in quality "very good." The sunny side is figured in the plate, the other is less inviting, but this blemish in its exterior appearance is fully compensated by its superior excellency. It is also an abundant bearer.

From Nature by A Hoffy.

DIX PEAR

DIX.

Synonyms—None.
Size of Fruit—From 3 to 3¾ inches by 2½ to 2¾.
Form—Long, obovate, pyriform, one side usually larger than the other.
Skin—Yellowish green, becoming deep yellow, some times a brown cheek, densely covered with large russet dots, giving to the exterior a rough appearance.
Stalk—Cinnamon color, from ⅞ to 1⅛ inches long, and from 1/12 to ⅛ thick, stouter at each end, inserted rather obliquely in a small irregular cavity, with sometimes a small prominence on one side.
Calyx—Below medium, segments closed, set in a small very superficial basin.
Core—Rather large.
Seed—Small, chestnut color, ⅜ long, 1/10 wide, ⅛ thick.
Flesh—Somewhat granular especially around the core, juice abundant.
Flavor—Rich, vinous, sprightly, with a delicate perfume.
Quality—"Best."
Maturity—October and November.
Leaf—Oval, acuminate, slightly serrate, 1¼ to 1¾ inches wide, by 3¾ to 4½ long, including petiole, which is from 1¼ to 2¼ inches long by 1/16 thick.
Wood—Young shoots, yellowish, slender, sometimes thorny. Old—olive brown.

HISTORY, ETC.

The Dix Pear is a native of Massachusetts. It originated in the garden of the late Dr. Dix, Washington Street, Boston, but did not come into bearing till after his death, which occurred in 1809. In 1825 it fruited for the first time.

The tree is often ten or fifteen years in coming into bearing, but is then a certain and abundant bearer.

It is one of the varieties of pears that does not succeed well on the quince, unless double worked. Mr. P. Barry has obtained a fine crop in two years by working it on the jargonelle or quince.

I. P. Cushing, Esq., of Watertown, from whom we received beautiful specimens of the fruit, regards it as one of the best of pears.

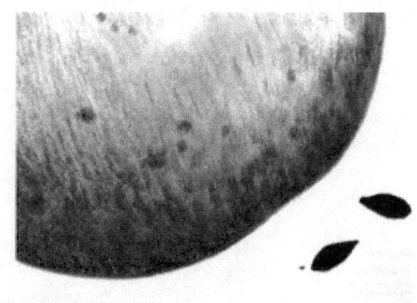

From Nature by A. Hoffy.

SMOKE HOUSE.

Synonyms—Millcreek, Vandervere.

Size of Fruit—Above medium. $\begin{cases} \text{Longitudinal diameter, } 2\frac{1}{4} \text{ inches.} \\ \text{Transverse diameter, } 3\frac{1}{4} \text{ inches.} \end{cases}$

Form—Oblate.

Skin—Striped and mottled with crimson, on a greenish-yellow ground.

Stem—½ to ¾ inches by $\frac{1}{1}\frac{}{7}$, curved, inserted in a rather narrow, not very deep cavity.

Calyx—Closed, set in a wide shallow basin.

Core—Medium.

Seed—Brown, long, acuminate, ⅜ inch long, ¼ wide, $\frac{1}{16}$ thick.

Flesh—Yellowish-white, crisp, juicy.

Flavor—Rich, sub-acid, with a peculiar delicate aroma.

Quality—"Very good."

Maturity—October to January.

Leaf—1½ inches wide, 3¼ long, including the petiole, which is ⅜ inch long, $\frac{1}{1}\frac{}{5}$ thick.

Wood—Young shoots, brown.

Growth—Moderately vigorous.

HISTORY, ETC.

The Smoke House is a native of Pennsylvania. It originated with William Gibbons, Lampeter Township, Lancaster County, and grew near his smoke-house. The variety was brought into notice, twenty or thirty years ago, by Mr. Ashbridge, though it had long before been in the nursery of Mr. Connard, who resided in the vicinity of its original locality. It is probably a natural Seedling from the Vandiver of Delaware.

From Nature by A. Hoffy.

HOWELL

HOWELL.

Synonyms—None.

Size of Fruit—{ Longitudinal diameter, 3 to 3½ inches.
Transverse diameter, 2¾ to 3¼ inches.

Form—Roundish, pyriform.

Skin—Yellow, many small russet dots and a few russet markings on the shaded side, often a faint blush on the side exposed to the sun, cavity russetted.

Stem—1 inch long, $\frac{2}{16}$ thick, curved a little fleshy at its insertion, which is oblique.

Calyx—Small, open, segments erect, set in a shallow, somewhat plaited basin.

Core—Medium.

Seed—Dark, ⅝ of an inch long, $\frac{2}{16}$ wide, ⅛ thick.

Flesh—Texture rather coarse, melting, juicy.

Flavor—Rich, sprightly, with a pleasant aroma.

Quality—"Very good."

Maturity—Last of September and October.

Leaf—1⅝ inches wide, 4¼ long, inclusive of petiole, which is 1¼ inches long, and $\frac{1}{16}$ thick.

Wood—Young shoots, olive.

Growth—Vigorous.

HISTORY, ETC.

The Howell is a native of Connecticut. It originated at New Haven, from seed planted by the late Mr. Thomas Howell in his garden, adjoining that of the late Governor Edwards.

The value of this fine Pear is greatly increased by its large size, and attractive exterior.

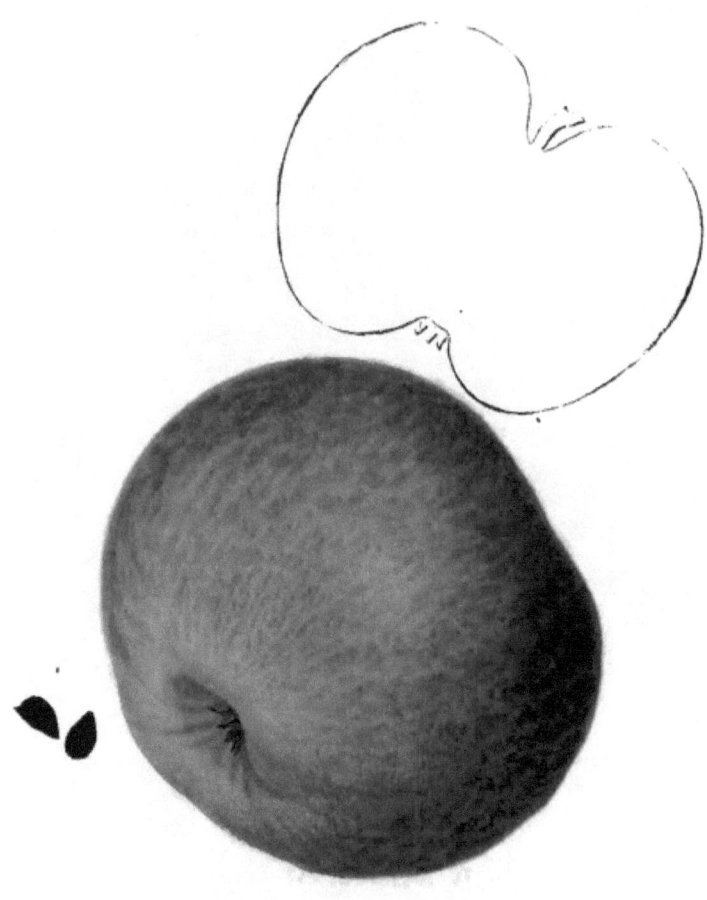

From Nature by A. Hoffy.

JEFFERIS.

JEFFERIES.

Synonyms—

Size of Fruit—Medium. $\begin{cases} \text{Longitudinal diameter, 2½ inches.} \\ \text{Transverse diameter, 3 inches.} \end{cases}$

Form—Roundish, oblate, inclining to conic.

Skin—With light and dark crimson on a yellow ground.

Stem—¼ to ½ inch long, slender, inserted in a deep open, slightly russeted cavity.

Calyx—Medium, segments woolly, nearly closed, set in a deep basin.

Core—Medium.

Seed—Dark brown, roundish, rather large.

Flesh—Yellowish white, tender, juicy.

Flavor—Very pleasant.

Quality—"Best."

Maturity—September.

Leaf—3½ by 1¾, including petiole, which is ¾ by ¹⁄₁₆.

Wood—Young shoots greenish brown, buds mealy.

Growth—Moderate, upright.

HISTORY, ETC.

The Jefferies is a native of Pennsylvania, and originated on the premises of Mr. Isaac Jefferies, Newlin Township, Chester County. It is a constant and abundant bearer.

The premium offered by the Pennsylvania Horticultural Society for the best seedling apple exhibited in 1848, was awarded to this variety, which was named by the Committee, the "Jefferies," after the originator.

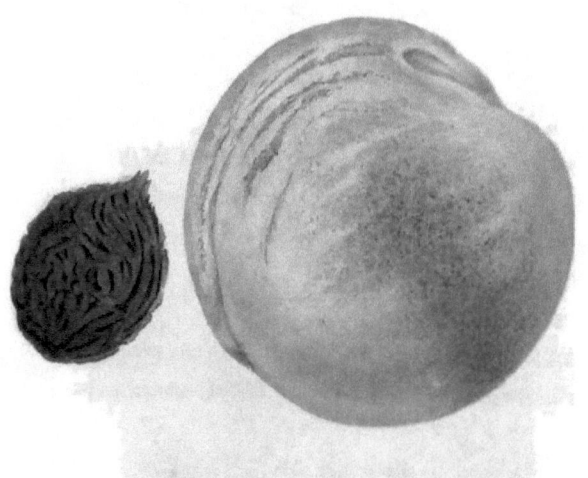

From Nature by A. Hoffy

GORGOS.

GORGAS.

Synonyms—None.

Size of Fruit—Rather large. { Longitudinal diameter, 2½ inches. Transverse diameter, 2¾ inches.

Form—Roundish, with a small swollen point at the apex.

Skin—Mellowed white, clouded and blotched with red on the exposed surface, dull greenish white on the shaded parts.

Suture—Indistinct.

Stem—Inserted in a deep, wide cavity.

Stone—Dark brownish yellow, 1$\frac{7}{8}$ inches long, 1 wide, ¾ thick.

Flesh—Whitish, slightly stained at the stone, juicy, non-adherent to the stone.

Flavor—Saccharine and exceedingly luscious.

Quality—"Best."

Maturity—About the 20th of September.

Leaf—Large, about 2 inches wide, 7¼ long, including the petiole, which is $\frac{7}{8}$ long, ⅛ thick, without glands, deeply serrate, folded, crimped along the mid-rib.

Blossom—Small.

Wood—Young, brownish-red on the sunny side.

Growth—Vigorous.

HISTORY, ETC.

The Gorgas Peach is a native of Pennsylvania. It originated with Benjamin Gullis, Pine Street above Broad, Philadelphia, from a stone of the Morris White, planted in the autumn of 1846. This variety fruited for the first time in 1850. In 1851, specimens of the fruit were exhibited at the Annual Exhibition of the Pennsylvania Horticultural Society.

SHELDON.

Synonyms—Bland, Huron, Mayne, Misner.
Size—Large, 2¾ to 3 inches long, by 3 to 3¼ wide, sometimes weighing 16 ounces.
Form—Usually roundish-obovate, sometimes obovate inclining to pyriform, occasionally truncate.
Skin—Green russet, becoming yellow russet, sometimes only faintly russeted, and very rarely a brownish red cheek.
Stem—Somewhat variable in size, usually ⅝ of an inch by ₁⁶₀, often ¾ by ⅛, occasionally 1 by ⅛, inserted sometimes obliquely in a narrow, superficial and occasionally in a rather deep cavity.
Calyx—Small, segments deeply cut, usually open, sometimes closed, often partially reflexed, set in a basin rather variable, usually shallow and narrow, sometimes wider and deeper.
Core—Medium.
Seed—Brown, small, ⅝ of an inch long, nearly ₁⁶₀ wide, ⅛ thick.
Flesh—Yellowish white, buttery, melting, abounding in juice, texture granular with grittiness round the core and extending to the stem and calyx.
Flavor—Rich, perfumed, with some resemblance to that of the Brown Beurré and Lodge.
Quality—"Very good."
Period of Maturity—October.
Leaf—2¾ inches long by 1¾ wide, exclusive of petiole which is 1¾ by ₁⁶₀.
Wood—Young shoots yellowish brown, old wood greyish brown.
Growth—Upright.

HISTORY, ETC.

The Sheldon Pear is a native of Wayne County, New York. The original tree stands in the town of Huron, on the premises of Major Sheldon, and sprung from seed planted by his father nearly forty years ago. Two other trees in the vicinity, one on the farm of Mr. Norman Sheldon, and the other on that of Mr. Wisner, are also said to be seedlings, bearing fruit very similar to the Sheldon. They have been carefully examined by competent pomologists, who assure us that they present no appearance of ever having been grafted or budded—and yet no one who has seen the fruit from these three trees can for a moment entertain a doubt as to their perfect and entire identity. The only way of reconciling the conflicting facts and statements of the case, is to adopt the more than probable conclusion that two of them are unmarked suckers from the remaining one. Such I have been credibly informed, is now the conviction of Major Sheldon.

A description of this variety was published in Hovey's Magazine of Horticulture for June, 1851, and in the Horticulturist for January, 1853.

From Nature by A. Hoffy.

NORTHERN SPY.

Synonyms—The Spy.
Size of Fruit— { Longitudinal diameter, 3¼ inches.
                  Transverse diameter, 3¼ inches.
Form—Roundish-conical, sometimes flattened, occasionally ribbed.
Skin—Striped and mottled, with red on a yellow ground.
Stalk—1 inch long, ¼ thick, inserted in deep, generally russetted cavity.
Calyx—Small, closed, set in a deep furrowed basin.
Core—Large.
Seed—Brown, abundant, ⅜ inches long, ⅛ wide, ¼ thick.
Flesh—Yellowish-white, fine texture, tender, juicy.
Flavor—Pleasant, sprightly, aromatic.
Quality—"Best."
Maturity—December to June.
Leaf—2½ inches wide, 6½ long, including petiole, which is 1¾ long by 1/5 thick.
Wood—Young shoots, reddish with many white dots, buds small; old wood, brownish-grey.
Growth—Rapid, erect.

HISTORY, ETC.

The Northern Spy is a native of New York. It originated in East Bloomfield, Ontario County, on the farm of Oliver Chapin, from seed brought from Connecticut some 40 years ago. During the past season I received beautiful specimens of this fine fruit from Mr. J. J. Thomas, Macedon, New York, and Mr. James H. Watts, Rochester. The latter gentleman in his letter to me remarks: "The tree is an upright, thrifty grower, and forms a close head, consequently it needs thorough trimming to give the fruit the benefit of the sun; without it, it never colors well, which is very necessary to develop the high flavor of which it is susceptible. He also remarks, that it does not put forth its "foliage" as early as other varieties by a fortnight, thus escaping late spring frosts.

From Nature by A Hoffy.

FREDERIKA BREMER.

Synonyms—Virgalieu, erroneously.

Size of Fruit— { Longitudinal diameter, 3 to 3¾ inches.
Transverse diameter, 2¾ to 3¼ inches.

Form—Irregularly obovate, often compressed at the sides, sometimes irregular in outline, with slight inequalities on the surface.

Skin—Fair, clear pale yellow, with some small russet dots.

Stalk—Yellow russet, 1⅜ inches long by $\frac{3}{16}$ thick, sometimes with fleshy rings at its insertion, usually inserted with little or no depression, occasionally in a small superficial irregular cavity, slightly russetted.

Calyx—Medium, closed, some of the segments now and then reflexed, set in a rather shallow, irregular basin.

Core—Medium.

Seed—Very dark, slight pointed at the anterior of the blunt extremity, ⅜ inch long, $\frac{3}{16}$ wide, ⅛ thick.

Flesh—Fine texture, buttery, melting.

Flavor—Rich and vinous.

Quality—"Best."

Maturity—October.

Leaf—Serratures acute, 1½ inches wide by 3 to 3½ long, inclusive of petiole, which is from ⅝ to 1 inch long by $\frac{1}{16}$ thick.

Wood—Young shoots brownish olive.

Growth—Moderate.

HISTORY, ETC.

The Frederika Bremer Pear originated in the State of New York, and was brought into notice by J. C. Hastings, Esq., of Clinton, Oneida County. In regard to its history, the following information was communicated to me in a letter from him in 1849:—"I have no doubt of its being a seedling; it having originated near me from seed brought from Connecticut about 40 years since; and I think it but little known in this vicinity, except in the immediate neighborhood of the original tree. My attention was first called to the Pear by seeing it offered for sale as the Virgalieu, a name which has been in common use for all Pears (from ordinary to good) in this region, until within a few years past. As I was about sending it to the Exhibition, I happened to say something about giving it a name, and a lady present immediately suggested the name of Frederika Bremer, one so much in accordance with my own feelings, that I did not hesitate to adopt it."

In a subsequent letter he adds: "I have known this Pear five or six years, and have been surprised to see it so uniformly, from year to year, well filled with fruit, always fair and of good size. Indeed, I know of no Pear that promises so well with us, except perhaps the Bartlett.

The first descriptions of this excellent variety were published in Hovey's Magazine for January, 1850, and the Horticulturist for March, 1850.

When the fruit has attained its complete maturity, it cannot ordinarily be kept long, as it is liable speedily to decay at the core, while presenting a fair exterior.

3

NORTH AMERICAN POMOLOGIST.

From Nature by A. Hoffy.

REPUBLICAN PIPPIN.

Size—Large, 2¾ to 3 inches long, by 3¾ to 4 inches in width.
Form—Oblate.
Skin—Striped with red on a mottled reddish ground, and when not exposed to the sun, of a greenish yellow with a few large gray dots.
Stem—About an inch long, slender for so large a fruit, inserted in a narrow, rather deep cavity, which is sometimes a little russetted, the russet patch diverging in rays.
Calyx—With small or narrow segments, closed, and set in a moderately deep basin.
Core—Small.
Seed—Brown, large, broad, plump.
Flesh—Yellowish-white, tender.
Flavor—Pleasant and peculiar, resembling somewhat that of Walnuts.
Maturity—September, October.
Leaf—Broad, dark green, somewhat plaited or rugose, serrate, under side glareous with reddish veins.
Wood—Dark reddish brown.

HISTORY, ETC.

A native of Pennsylvania. The original tree was discovered in the woods near Muncy, Lycoming County, in 1796, by George Webb, by whom it was extensively propagated. The tree is still standing in its original locality, and in vigorous health. Scions were sent to England in 1827, to J. H. Lewis, Esq., of East Farleigh, Kent, who now has trees of it bearing. On the authority of Dr. Kittee, of Lycoming County, "it is fit for cooking the last of July. For drying it cannot be surpassed, cooking to a fine pulp in a very short time. In the green state it cooks well, and has a delicious flavor. The tree grows vigorously on any soil, but does not bear well on limestone land. It has a crop every year."

This variety is cultivated to some extent in the vicinity of Westchester, in this State, where it sustains its high character.

from Nature by A. Hoffy.

COLUMBIA.

Synonyms—Columbia Virgalieu, Columbia Virgouleuse.

Size of Fruit—Large $\begin{cases} \text{Longitudinal diameter } 3\frac{3}{8} \text{ inches.} \\ \text{Transverse diameter } 3\frac{1}{4} \text{ inches.} \end{cases}$

Form—Round, obovate, usually one sided.

Skin—Smooth, fair, pale green, becoming lemon yellow, with minute russet dots, and sometimes a few interrupted russet streaks.

Stem—1¼ inches long by ⅜ thick, becoming more stout and fleshy at its junction with the spur or branch, usually curved, inserted obliquely in a small narrow cavity.

Core—Medium.

Seed—Light cinnamon, acuminate, ½ inch long ₁⁄₁₆ wide, ⅛ thick, with an angle at one side of the blunt end.

Flesh—White, granular near the core, melting and buttery.

Flavor—Rich, saccharine, with an agreeable aroma.

Quality—"Very good" sometimes "best."

Maturity—From November to January.

Leaf—1¼ to 1¾ inches wide by 3½ to 4¼ long, including petiole, which is 1¼ to 2¼ inches in length to 1¼ in width.

Wood—Young shoots brownish yellow, old wood grey olive.

Growth—Upright, vigorous.

HISTORY, ETC.

The Columbia Pear is a native of West Chester County, New York. It originated on the farm of Mr. Casser, thirteen miles from the City of New York; and was brought into notice by Bloodgood & Co., of Flushing, Long Island.

Hon. M. P. Wilder remarks in the Horticulturist, (Vol. 1, page 20.) "This excellent native variety has proved with me a fruit more uniformly smooth, perfect in shape, and free from the depredations of insects, than almost any other sort." He esteems it one of the five best winter Pears; the other four being Beurré d'Aremberg, Winter Nelis, Glout Morceau and Passe Colmar. It is an abundant bearer when the trees have arrived at a mature age.

From Nature by A. Hoffy

ELIZA PEACH.

Size—Large.

Form—Round, terminating in a nipple.

Skin—Yellow, with a mottled red cheek.

Flesh—Yellow, red at the stone.

Flavor—Very fine.

Maturity—Last of September.

Stone—Not adhering.

Leaf—Large, with reniform glands.

HISTORY, ETC.

This Peach was raised on the premises of Mr. Gerard Schmitz, South Fifth Street, in the District of Southwark. It received the premium offered by the Pennsylvania Horticultural Society for the best Seedling Peach exhibited in 1849.

From Nature by A. Hoffy

BLOODGOOD.

Synonyms—Early Buerre of some.

Size— { Longitudinal diameter $2\frac{1}{8}$ to $2\frac{1}{4}$ inches.
Transverse diameter $2\frac{1}{8}$ to $2\frac{1}{4}$ inches.

Form—Roundish, obovate, sometimes turbinate, usually contracted or tapering at the crown.

Skin—Yellow, dotted and marbled with russet.

Stalk—Cinnamon color, somewhat variable in size, from $\frac{5}{8}$ to 1 inch long by $\frac{1}{8}$ to $\frac{3}{16}$ in thickness, fleshy at its insertion, which is oblique without depression.

Calyx—Medium, segments reflected, set in a shallow, narrow, sometimes irregular basin.

Core—Below medium.

Seed—Dark, $\frac{3}{8}$ long, $\frac{3}{16}$ wide, $\frac{1}{8}$ thick.

Flesh—Whiteish, buttery and melting.

Flavor—Rich, with a delightful aroma.

Quality—"Very good."

Maturity—Beginning to middle of August.

Leaf—Usually flat, oval, terminating abruptly in an acute point, serratures crenate, $1\frac{11}{16}$ inches wide, and $3\frac{11}{16}$ long, including petiole, which is $1\frac{1}{16}$ of an inch long by $\frac{1}{16}$ thick.

Wood—Young shoots reddish brown, short jointed.

Growth—Upright, moderately vigorous.

HISTORY, ETC.

The origin of the Bloodgood Pear is enveloped in mystery. About the year 1835, scions of it were left at the nursery of Mr. James Bloodgood, of Flushing, by a stranger, who represented it as a new variety. Being found to possess much merit, it was extensively disseminated by Mr. Bloodgood, and received his name.

The fine variety succeeds well on the Quince, and like all summer Pears, house ripening is required to have it in the greatest perfection.

From Nature by A. Hoffy.

CUSHING RASPBERRY

CUSHING RASPBERRY.

Size—Rather large.

Form—Roundish, conical.

Color—Crimson.

Flavor—Fine and sprightly.

Maturity—June and sometimes October.

Leaf—Much plaited, and regular in form.

Stalk—With brown spines.

HISTORY, ETC.

This new Raspberry was named in honor of I. P. Cushing, Esq., of Watertown, Mass. It was produced from a seed of the new double bearing, which had been imported by Mr. Robert Buist, of this city. The seed was planted, June 27th, 1843, and vegetated in the Spring of the following year. It fruited for the first time in the Autumn of 1845, only one berry however matured at that time, in consequence of the accession of cold weather. Besides fruiting in the summer, it invariably makes an effort to produce a second crop in October; and not unfrequently the effort proves successful. The October crop is always produced on the wood grown the same season, and not on that of the preceding year. In 1850 the second crop commenced on the 20th of October, and in November following a branch with ripe fruit on it, was cut off, and exhibited at the meeting of the Pennsylvania Horticultural Society.

OTT.

Synonyms—Ott's Seedling.
Size of Fruit—Rather small. $\begin{cases} \text{Longitudinal diameter, 2 to } 2\frac{1}{4} \text{ inches.} \\ \text{Transverse diameter, } 1\frac{7}{8} \text{ to } 2\frac{1}{2} \text{ inches.} \end{cases}$

In 1859 this Pear was grown at Grovehill, measuring $2\frac{3}{4}$ by $2\frac{1}{2}$ inches.

Form—Roundish, obovate, sometimes inclining to turbinate, and usually flattened at the crown.
Skin—Greenish yellow, considerably russeted, often stained and marbled with red on the exposed side, especially towards the crown.
Stem—Cinnamon color, $1\frac{1}{4}$ inches long, $\frac{1}{8}$ thick, usually curved, and inserted with little or no depression.
Calyx—Rather large, segments reflexed, set in a shallow basin.
Core—Small.
Seed—Black, $\frac{5}{16}$ inch long, $\frac{3}{16}$ wide, $\frac{1}{8}$ thick, with a prominent point or angle on the inner side of the blunt end.
Flesh—Whitish yellow, somewhat granular, buttery, melting.
Flavor—Rich and saccharine, with an aroma very similar to that of its parent, the Seckel.
Quality—"Best."
Period of Maturity—August.
Leaf—Flat, $1\frac{1}{2}$ to $2\frac{1}{4}$ inches wide, $3\frac{1}{2}$ to $4\frac{1}{2}$ long, including the petiole, which is from $\frac{3}{4}$ to 2 inches long, by $\frac{1}{16}$ thick.
Wood—Young shoots, olive—old wood, ferruginous.
Growth—Rather vigorous.

HISTORY, ETC.

The Ott is a native of Pennsylvania. It originated with the late Mr. Samuel Ott, of Lower Merion Township, Montgomery County, from a seed of the Seckel planted in 1836. The Pennsylvania Horticultural Society awarded to this variety the premium offered for the best Seedling Pear exhibited in 1848, and gave to it its present name. It is not surpassed in quality by any summer pear we have. The first description of the Ott was published in the third volume of the Horticulturist.

From Nature by A. Hoffy.

COL. WILDER RASPBERRY.

Size—Large.
Form—Roundish, semi-transparent, varnished, prominent pips.
Color—Yellowish white or a delicate cream color.
Flavor—Very fine.
Maturity—June.
Leaf—Much crimped.
Stalk—With white spines.

HISTORY, ETC.

This variety originated from a seed of the Fastolf, planted in the Spring of 1846. It was named in honor of my highly valued and distinguished friend, the late President of the Massachusetts Horticultural Society. It fruited in 1847, the year after the seed had been planted. The Col. Wilder is one of the finest flavored Raspberries, and a most profuse bearer. Its semi-transparent, glazed and prominent pips, render its appearance peculiarly beautiful and attractive. Many seedlings have been raised from this variety, some bearing fruit similar in every respect to that of the parent, others fruit of a yellow color, not unlike the yellow Antwerp and many crimson fruit.

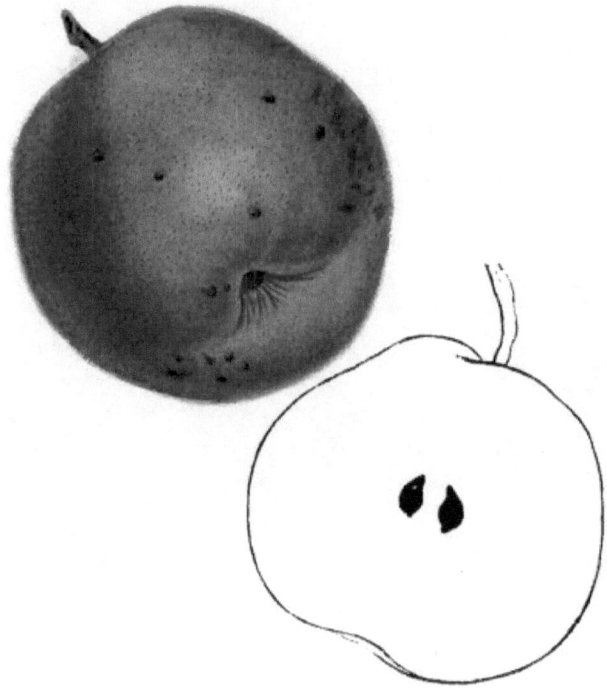

From Nature by A. Haffy

STYER.

Synonyms—

Size of Fruit—{ Longitudinal diameter, 2⅜ to 2¾ inches.
Transverse diameter, 2⅜ to 2¾ inches.

Form—Roundish.
Skin—Green, becoming yellow, with many russet dots and markings.
Stem—¾ inch long, 1/16 to ⅛ thick, inserted in a small shallow cavity.
Calyx—Almost obsolete, basin narrow, moderately deep.
Core—Medium.
Seed—Very dark brown, short, rather plump, 5/16 inch long, 3/16 wide, 3/16 thick, slight prominence or angle on one side of the blunt extremity.
Flesh—Yellowish white, granular, somewhat gritty at the core, buttery and melting.
Flavor—Exceedingly rich, and highly perfumed.
Quality—"Best."
Maturity—Beginning of September.
Leaf—Oval, recurved, 1⅜ inches wide, 4¼ long, including petiole, which is 1⅜ inches long by 1/16 thick, and at its junction with the branch, ⅛.
Wood—Young shoots, brownish yellow; old, grey.

HISTORY, ETC.

The Styer is believed to be a native of Pennsylvania. My attention was directed to this variety by Alexander W. Corson, Esq., to whom I am indebted for specimens of the fruit, and for the subjoined information in regard to its history.

About twenty years ago, Mr. Charles Styer, of Whitplain Township, Montgomery County, some fifteen miles from Philadelphia, engaged a man to make a fence for him, Mr. Styer happened at the time to say something about having some pear stocks grafted; on hearing which, the fence-maker said he knew where there was a fine kind, and would bring him some of the scions. He accordingly procured the scions, and they were inserted; but it was never known where he obtained them, and he died without imparting this information. From these grafted trees the variety has been propagated to some extent in that neighborhood.

The Styer is represented to be an abundant bearer of fair and perfect fruit, which commands a high price in the market.

Specimens of the fruit were exhibited at the meeting of the American Pomological Society at Philadelphia in September, 1852, and after a careful examination, the quality was decided by the Committee on Native Fruits, to be "best."

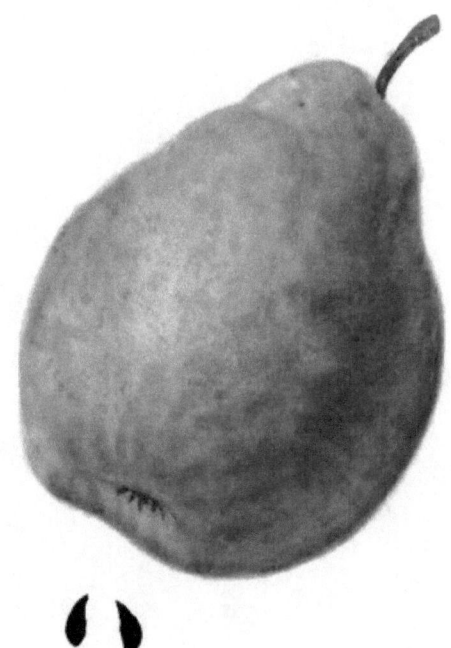

From Nature by A Baffy.

PETRE PEAR

PETRE.

Size—Full medium.

Form—Obovate.

Skin—Pale yellow, with sometimes russet patches.

Stem—About an inch long, rather stout, inserted in depression usually flattened.

Calyx—Small, set in a narrow basin.

Flesh—Whiteish, of fine texture and buttery consistence.

Flavor—Rich and perfumed.

Maturity—September.

Wood—Yellowish brown, older wood olive brown, shoots slender.

HISTORY, ETC.

This fine Autumn Pear, originated from a seed of the White Doyenne from London, to the elder John Bartram, by Lady Petre, in 1735. The original tree, now about 125 years old, is yet standing at the Bartram Garden, near the southeast corner of the old mansion. This variety is of rather slow growth, but bears most abundantly and uniformly a crop of fine fruit. Several of the Seedlings raised by Bartram from the Petre, still remain on the premises; the Chapman, however, is the only one that possesses any merit.

From Nature by A. Hoffy.

BRANDYWINE PEAR

BRANDYWINE PEAR.

Size—Medium, 2¾ inches long by 2 in width.
Form—Pyriform, much flattened at the base.
Skin—Yellowish Green, nearly covered with russet dots and blotches, especially around the eye.
Stem—One inch long, medium thickness, somewhat fleshy at its insertion, without depression.
Calyx—Of Medium size, open, set in a wide shallow basin.
Core—Rather small.
Seed—Dark brown.
Flesh—White, melting.
Flavor—Rich, resembling in Mr. Downing's opinion, that of the white Doyenne and Marie Louise, combined.
Maturity—Middle of August.
Leaf—Rather long, slender, serrate.
Wood—Yellowish olive, interspersed with white dots.
Tree—A free grower—a regular abundant bearer.

HISTORY, ETC.

Dr. Ellwood Harvey, of Chaddsford, gives in the 3d Vol. Horticulturist, the following history of this fine new Pennsylvania Pear.

"The original Tree was found near a fence in a field on my father's farm, (the late Eli Harvey.) It was transplanted when quite small, to a garden on the property of George Brinton, then owned by his grandfather, Caleb Brinton. This garden on the banks of the Brandywine River, is a part of the ground on which the American Army stood in the defence of our Country in the Battle of Brandywine; and I therefore respectfully suggest the above name as an appropriate one for the fruit. The tree began to bear fruit about the year 1820, and in 1835 the original trunk blew down near the surface of the ground. The present tree is a sucker or shoot, which sprang up from the root, and has now been in bearing four or five years."

I saw this Pear for the first time in the Summer of 1848. It and another variety were sent to me from Westchester before a description of it was published in the Horticulturist, for the purpose of obtaining my opinion of their merits. I unhesitatingly pronounced the Brandywine to be greatly superior to the other, and to be a fruit of the first quality.

From Nature by A. Hoffy.

MOYAMENSING PEAR

MOYAMENSING.

Size—Full medium.

Form—Round obovate, somewhat irregular.

Skin—Lemon yellow, with occasionally blotches and lines of russet.

Stem—Variable, usually about an inch long, fleshy.

Calyx—Rather small, set in a furrowed basin.

Flesh—Buttery, melting.

Flavor—Very pleasant.

Maturity—August.

Leaf—Medium size, petioles rather long.

Wood—Yellowish brown, with numerous white dots.

HISTORY, ETC.

This fine Summer Pear originated in the garden of the late J. B. Smith, Esq., of Philadelphia. His residence being in the District of Moyamensing, induced the Pennsylvania Horticultural Society in 1845 to name it Smith's Moyamensing. The original tree is seventy or eighty years old, and has always been a constant and uniform bearer.

From Nature by A Roffy

PENNSYLVANIA.

Size—Above medium.

Form—Short, obovate.

Skin—Brownish russet on yellowish ground.

Stem—1½ long, 1/10th in width, inserted in a slight depression.

Calyx—Small set in a shallow basin.

Flesh—Rather course, half melting.

Flavor—Highly perfumed.

Maturity—Beginning of September.

Wood—Young wood, reddish brown.

Tree—Vigorous, diverging.

HISTORY, ETC.

The Pennsylvania Pear originated some fifty or sixty years ago, in the garden of the late John B. Smith, in the district of Moyamensing. The name was given to it by the Pennsylvania Horticultural Society. The original tree, of large size, is still remaining on the premises in Christian Street, and is within twenty or thirty feet of the Moyamensing Pear. In some parts of Ohio, another Pear is cultivated under this name.

CONTENTS

OF THE

NORTH AMERICAN POMOLOGIST.

BOOK No. 1.

APPLES.

CHELTENHAM
CLYDE BEAUTY
JEFFERIS
NORTHERN SPY
NORTHERN SWEET
REPUBLICAN PIPPIN
SMOKE HOUSE

BURLINGTON APRICOT

WILMINGTON CHESTNUT

WENDELL'S MOTTLED BIGARREAU

DIANA GRAPE

PEACHES.

ELIZA
GORGAS
JANE
PENELOPE

PEARS.

BLOODGOOD
BRANDYWINE
CHANCELLOR
COLUMBIA
DIX
FREDERIKA BREMER
HEATHCOT
HOWEL
LAWRENCE
MOYAMENSING
OTT
PENNSYLVANIA
PETRE
SECKEL
SHELDON
STYER

PLUMS.

CLEAVINGER
GENERAL HAND

RASPBERRIES.

CUSHING
ORANGE
COL. WILDER

www.ingramcontent.com/pod-product-compliance
Lightning Source LLC
Chambersburg PA
CBHW030354170426
43202CB00010B/1367